Dog Cancer:
The Holistic Answer

A Step by Step Guide

Dr. Steven Eisen
www.DogCancerAdvice.com

Dr. Steven Eisen
ISBN: 1-4515-1883-8
ISBN-13: 9781451518832

Dedication

This book is dedicated to Fergie Eisen
December 16, 1994 – April 28, 2008

*"He is your friend, your partner, your defender, your dog.
You are his life, his love, his leader. He will be yours, faithful
and true, to the last beat of his heart. You owe it to him to be
worthy of such devotion."—Unknown*

Table of Contents

Introduction: One Case Among Millions vii

How to Use This Book xiii

1   You Can Cure Your Dog 1

2   Getting Reliable Information 7

3   Conventional and Non-Conventional
    Cancer treatments 13
    Weighing Options 13
    Costs 15
    Effectiveness 16
    Quality of Life 17
    A New Wonder Drug? .19
    Practicality 20
    Assumptions 21

4   Step One: Removing Poisons 25
    Commercial Dog Food 26
    Bacteria 26
    Drugs 27
    Mycotoxins 27
    Chemical Residue 28

GMOs. 28
Acrylamide 28
Nutria 30
Water 31
Household Chemicals 34
Flea and Tick Products 34
Pesticides and Herbicides. 37
Liquid Zeolite 39
Stress 40

5   <u>Step Two</u>: The Dog Cancer Diet 43

6   <u>Step Three</u>: Immune Enhancement. 51
Avemar 51
AHCC 53
Beta Glucan 54

7   <u>Step Four</u>: Enzyme Therapy 57

8   <u>Step Five</u>: Vitamins, Herbs and
Other Considerations 63
Other Supplements 64
Homeopathic Remedies 66
Dosages. 68
Energy Treatments 68

9   Testing 71
Practicing the Test. 73
Using the Test 76

10 A Last Word – to Fergie. 79

Introduction

One Case Among Millions

As in humans, the incidence of cancer in dogs is dramatically rising. According to the American Society for the Prevention of Cruelty to Animals (ASPCA), 60% of all dogs over age six will be diagnosed with some type of cancer in their lifetime. About six million dogs are diagnosed with cancer each year in the United States, according to the National Cancer Institute (NCI). Dogs have thirty-five times more skin cancer than do humans, four times more breast tumors, eight times more bone cancer, and twice the incidence of leukemia. Cancer is the number one killer of dogs over the age of two.

Chances are, you are reading this because your dog has been diagnosed with cancer. If so, you are most likely going through great emotional distress and looking for reliable information about what remedies are available.

Such was the case with my wife and me a few years ago. Fergie, our beloved Lhasa Apso, had had a tumorous spleen surgically removed, but her prognosis was grim.

My mother had died of cancer in 2001, after suffering heroically through the toxic side effects of conventional treatments. This had set me on a mission to learn as much as I could about alternative approaches to the disease. I came to this research as a Doctor of Chiropractic, well schooled in physiology but with much to learn about the nature and behavior of cells run rampant.

Just as most people think it's prudent not to wait until the day they retire to figure out how they are going to pay their bills when their employment ends, it makes sense to prepare for the possibility of cancer long before we might receive a diagnosis. More than a third of us will be touched by some form of cancer in our lifetime. With luck, you and I will be among the majority that's spared. But if we aren't, and if we have to make a rapid decision about how to respond, the chance of our choosing the best option will obviously be greater if we have made some effort to educate ourselves about the disease in advance.

So, in the couple of years before Fergie's diagnosis, I had spent countless hours reading books, listening and talking to experts, and in other ways assembling a knowledge base about conventional and non-conventional cancer treatments, as well as the politics of cancer. This meant that, when we were told Fergie would probably not live for more than six weeks without intervention, I had a huge head start.

My challenge was to take all I had learned about human cancer and apply it to treating a dog. I was primarily interested in alternative treatments. What I had to assess was which of these could be adapted to Fergie, and then which seemed to have the highest chance of success.

Part of this investigation involved joining internet discussion groups to find out what other people were doing and what they knew. To my dismay, I found that most dog owners were pretty much in the dark. They were starved for information and had only a small fraction of the knowledge that I had been able to accumulate. Fragments of understanding popped up here and there, but nothing that could be considered a comprehensive, reliable strategy for treating a dog's cancer.

Many participants in the discussion groups were treating their pets with a single product claimed by its marketers to be the answer to canine cancer. They hoped they had found the magic bullet – a perfect remedy that works in all cases. Unfortunately, no such remedy exists. Others were using more than one substance, but they were blindly trying to guess their way to a cure. I'm sure some of these attempts were accidentally successful. I recently went back to some of the discussion groups to see if anything had changed. Sadly, confusion and wishful thinking still reigned

I set out to develop a comprehensive protocol for Fergie based on the best information I had gathered up to that point. The results more than fulfilled my hopes: she lived another two years, four months, and eighteen days. Veterinarians consider canine cancer to be in complete remission (cured) if there is no sign of recurrence for *eight months*. With conventional chemotherapy, there would have been no expectation of a cure; the prognosis for Fergie was nine to twelve months, and her quality of life would have been markedly reduced by the treatment. Our vet was amazed by the success of our alternative protocol, saying she had never seen any dog with Fergie's diagnosis live so long and so well.

After two years, Fergie began to have epileptic seizures, which increased in frequency over the last few months of her life. We suspect that the cancer had metastasized to her brain, but we will never know for sure because no MRI was performed. If Fergie had a brain tumor, surgical removal may have been possible, but we would never have consented to it. We could not have subjected our little dog to such a traumatic – and risky – procedure. Besides, Fergie was nearly halfway through her fourteenth year, which is considered normal life expectancy for her breed.

But, as successful as we were, I now strongly believe that we could have done more. Further research and personal experiences over the last couple of years have enlarged my understanding of non-conventional cancer treatments. Also, I now see that, in my certainty that the cancer was cured, I let my guard down and did not keep up with some of the protocols that could have prevented metastasis. In this book, I have revised my original protocols with that in mind.

There are many supplements and products mentioned in the following pages. For your convenience, I have set up a companion website that will link you directly to sources for each of these items, at the best prices currently available. Using this website, www.bestdog-cures.com, will save you a considerable amount of time. Hereafter, I will refer to it as BDC.

You have choices in the treatment of your dog. Whatever course you choose, I will respect your decision. I just ask that you educate yourself sufficiently before deciding how to proceed. I have done my best to provide you with the essential information and guidance you will need. I also encourage you to read other books about cancer when you have the time.

No matter what the situation you are confronting right now, I send you my very best wishes and my absolute confidence that your dog will benefit from the advice you will find in these pages.

Dr. Steven Eisen
Venice, Florida
June 2009

How to Use This Book

In this book, I describe five "steps" in the healing of a dog with cancer. However, you should not feel that this is an all-or-nothing program. The one essential step is the first, "Removing Poisons," since it would be pointless to take any other steps while you are still exposing your dog to toxins. Beyond that, you may pick and choose among the steps, according to your needs and circumstances. On the other hand, the more you do the better. The steps have a cumulative effect, each building upon the last.

The first three chapters contain background information, which may be skipped if you have an immediate need to get to work on the cancer cure. The steps are detailed in Chapters 4-8, while a valuable method for sorting through your options for supplements is described in Chapter 9.

Note: the initials "BDC" refer to the website www. bestdogcures.com.

You can also sign up for our newsletter and more at www.dogcanceradvice.com.

Chapter 1
You Can Cure Your Dog

The evening of December 9th, 2005 was a cold one in Blue Bell, Pennsylvania. My wife, Leslee, and I were working on our computers in our home office while Fergie, our "baby," as we used to call her, was sitting by my wife on the floor. In just seven days, we would be celebrating her eleventh birthday. She had been acting strangely lately, as if something was bothering her, but we couldn't quite figure out what it was.

All dog owners know when their canine companions want something; the signals are unmistakable. When dogs are eager to go outside, they will typically stand at the door and whimper or bark. When they are hungry, they will come up and gaze into your eyes with a longing look, then lead you to the kitchen or their food bowl. Fergie, like many dogs, loved cookies. She frequently begged for them by coming up to us, lightly growling, and motioning with eyes and body toward the kitchen, where the cookies were kept.

However, for the past couple of months, we had clearly been failing to read Fergie's communications.

We would respond to her uncharacteristically vague requests by taking her out, giving her cookies, feeding her, or providing whatever else we thought she might need. No matter what we did, she remained unsatisfied and continued her petitions. Finally, we found out what she was trying to tell us.

At 9:30 on that chilly night in Blue Bell, Fergie suddenly collapsed at Leslee's feet. In a panic, Leslee called out to me. "Steven, oh my God! Come here, something's wrong with Fergie!" I rushed over to see what was happening. Nothing like this had ever happened before. Something must be seriously wrong. Was our beloved girl dying? What was going on? Our heads teemed with speculations.

I told Leslee we needed to get to an emergency veterinarian immediately. We reached for the yellow pages and found the closest clinic, which was almost thirty minutes away. I scooped Fergie up from the floor and rushed her out to the car. She was limp and lifeless, but still breathing.

When we got to the clinic, Fergie was awake and slightly more animated. I carried her in, and she started walking around as if nothing had happened. After filling out the paperwork, we were led into the examination room where the vet told us that Fergie needed to be kept overnight for observation and testing.

Early the next morning, when we went back to the clinic, we were told that they hadn't found anything abnormal in the blood work, but an X-ray had revealed something suspicious in the spleen. They recommended an ultrasound. However, it was explained to us that, whatever the findings of the ultrasound, exploratory surgery was already indicated. Since I didn't see any point in spending an additional $200 on a test that wouldn't contribute any unique information to diagnosis or treatment, I declined it. The clinic then contacted our regular vet, and arrangements were made to perform the surgery at 4:00 that afternoon.

We met with the vet at 3:00, and she showed us the X-ray. Fergie had a tumor in her spleen; she had probably collapsed the night before because the spleen had ruptured and she was bleeding internally. The vet went on to tell us that the only way to find out exactly what was going on was to open the dog up and look inside. She said that sometimes they would find the cancer to be so widespread, it was advisable to put the dog down. Alternatively, if there had been no spread, they could remove the tumor and hope for a good recovery. The vet added that we also had the option of bypassing the surgery and euthanizing Fergie immediately.

We couldn't bear the thought of not doing everything in our power to save Fergie, so euthanasia at this point was ruled out. The vet said that if she found widespread cancer, she would call us in the middle of the operation to ask if we were ready to take that step.

The vet left the room so that we could be alone with our little girl. Would these be our last moments with her? We cried and told her how much we loved her and that we were going to do what was best for her. We thanked her and said how grateful we were for her unconditional love over the years and the wondrous things she had done for us. She kissed our faces. We said goodbye, called for the veterinary assistant to take her, and sadly watched as she was carried away.

Family crises never happen at a good time. Leslee and I had recently purchased a new home in Florida and were scheduled to move in five days. Would we be moving without our precious Fergie? As John Lennon wrote, "Life is what happens to you while you're busy making other plans." This was definitely not in our plans.

At 4:00 p.m., we sat near the phone in our living room and waited. I told my wife to hope it wouldn't ring. The more time that passed without the phone ringing, the better the chances were that Fergie would live.

I paced back and forth, as I often do when I'm nervous. Leslee sat on the sofa. We wept, we worried, we prayed. Would our precious gift be taken away from us? Were our happy times with her over?

Five o'clock arrived. No phone call. I wanted to think that was good, but still couldn't relax. The digits advanced:

5:10 . . . 5:15 . . . 5:20 . . . 5:30 . . . Silence. The more minutes that passed without the phone ringing, the more hopeful I allowed myself to be. Certainly the operation was well under way. By this time, they would surely have found any scattering of the cancer. At 5:55, the phone finally rang. I grabbed it. The veterinary assistant said the spleen and its tumor had been removed and the vet was sewing Fergie back up.

I hung up and shouted with joy, "Fergie's coming to Florida with us!" Leslee and I hugged and cried. Things were going to be OK, it seemed.

Fergie remained in the pet hospital for a couple of days, recovering. On December 15th, we gleefully put her in the car and set off for Florida. Life was good again.

Fergie's tumor, like any other that is surgically removed, was sent to a lab for a biopsy so that it could be properly identified. About ten days after the operation, we were notified that it was a lymphosarcoma. I immediately went to the computer and googled "lymphosarcoma dogs." What I found was not good. The prognosis was survival for only four to eight weeks, and we were already halfway through the second week.

This news, once again, stirred up the fear of losing Fergie and caused me to muster all of my mental and emotional strength. I had been seriously studying alternative cancer treatments for a couple of years and was becoming an expert on the subject. Of course, my focus had been treatments for humans, but I knew I could adapt some of them to animal cancer.

After a little more research, I changed Fergie's diet and put her on a multi-pronged regimen of nutritional supplements specifically targeted on cancer.

The only conventional option for Fergie after her surgery was chemotherapy, which would have given her up to twelve more months of life, made hellish by diarrhea, vomiting, and other side effects. (It's worth noting here that, if a dog lives for eight months on chemotherapy, this is considered a cure, even if the animal dies days later. No, I'm not making this up!)

Fergie lived for another two years, four months, and eighteen days, with a good quality of life. That's equivalent to about eighteen human years. Fergie was thirteen years and four months old when she finally passed. That's normal life expectancy for a Lhasa Apso.

As I told our story to friends and acquaintances over the past couple of years, and helped many of them with dogs that had cancer, they all told me that I should write a book to share my discoveries with other dog owners facing a similar challenge. This is that book.

Just as Fergie was cured, your dog can be, too. There is hope based on solid facts. You will find all the necessary details in the following pages.

Chapter 2
Getting Reliable Information

There is an overwhelming amount of information regarding cancer treatments, online and elsewhere. However, you will find little guidance on how to assess or integrate all this material, much of which is of questionable origin. You could devote hundreds of hours to research and still have no clear idea about how best to proceed.

If your dog has cancer, you will have to make some crucial decisions over the next few days or weeks. You can't afford to lose precious time on a Google marathon that may lead you up scores of blind alleys. Your need is for a dependable strategy *right now*.

Over the past few years I have been asked for advice by people who knew of our success in curing Fergie. The following email is an example:

Hi Steven,
My dog's father has cancer. I know that you successfully prolonged the life of your dog and wondered if you could share what you did. He is a 13-year-old American Eskimo and had

a large tumor (sarcoma) removed from his abdomen within the last few months. In the last week, his abdomen blew up like a balloon. He has been drained twice. The vet has him on lasix and antibiotics. He is getting wheat grass, blue green algae and was going to get some essiac yesterday.

Any suggestions?

The treatment described had little chance of curing the dog's cancer. Like so many people, the sender of this email was just doing her best—and grasping at straws. She didn't know any better. And why would she? Solid information is both hard to find and bewildering when found.

If you have already done some research on alternative approaches to canine cancer, you may have come across the following arguments supporting recommended treatments:

"Based on scientific research." Scientific research can give us information that is valuable; however, again, it does not address the individual differences of different dogs. There is very little scientific research on non-conventional treatments for dogs with cancer. In addition, as you will see in the following pages, many studies are seriously flawed, and can be manipulated to produce false results.

"Confirmed by impressive testimonials." Making treatment choices based on testimonials is hazardous. Even a treatment with a measly 5% success rate may draw some

enthusiastic testimonials. You would never know from reading them that the treatment failed in 95% of the cases! Further, because of the individuality of every dog, the successes of one group of owners are not necessarily relevant to another owner. There is no universal magic bullet. Treatment *must* be individualized.

"It worked for a friend." The same objection about individuality applies here, but with even greater force. What can be learned from a sample of one?

Let's take a closer look at the scientific research that has been done on cancer in dogs.

A search of veterinary journals listed in the National Library of Medicine yields very little information about the causes of canine cancer, though there are many articles about conventional treatments such as chemotherapy and radiation.

One of the few studies that addresses causes is "Prevalence of obese dogs in a population of dogs with cancer," in the *American Journal of Veterinary Research*. It shows that dogs that had a history of corticosteroid use (corticosteroid drugs include prednisone, hydrocortisone, and triamcinolone) had higher rates of cancer, and those dogs were fatter from the steroid use. When the corticosteroid dogs were separated out, the remaining dogs with cancer had a lower incidence of excess weight.

Other findings were that the prevalence of cancer was higher in neutered dogs, both male and female, and that certain breeds were more at risk than others.

Surprisingly, the study found that higher body fat may be protective against certain types of cancer. (Mast cell tumors were an exception to this pattern.)

What does all this tell us? First, it tells us that we should shun corticosteroids for our dogs at all costs; there are more natural alternatives. It also tells us that neutering increases the risk of cancer. Neither this study nor other studies, however, shed light on how obesity is related, or not, to cancer in dogs.

Scientific research is not always the gold standard of reliability. Perhaps you remember that studies of the anti-inflammatory drug Vioxx were manipulated to show that it was safe and effective. The researchers wanted to suppress the fact that the drug caused heart attacks in some subjects. Their solution was simple: anyone who died wasn't counted! There are many, many studies that are just as deceptive.

You might seek guidance from "common knowledge" and clinical evidence. It's common knowledge, for example, that if a dog drinks antifreeze it will die. There is no scientific study on that, nor would it be humane to conduct one. Rather, the fact is established from clinical observation.

Of course, you could turn to your veterinarian. Most veterinarians are caring professionals who do the best they can with the resources available to them. But it's hardly reassuring that there are no published protocols or standards of care for canine cancer. In other words, each vet has to improvise his or her approach to a case. Your vet may suggest that you consult a veterinary oncologist, who will probably favor chemotherapy and/or radiation – expensive and, in my opinion, ineffective measures.

Some veterinarians describe themselves as "holistic." These practitioners will be supportive of the types of treatment discussed in this book. You can find such a vet by consulting a database maintained by the American Holistic Veterinary Medical Association at http://www.holisticvetlist.com.

Perhaps the most reliable information comes from specific testing of the individual dog. When a blood test shows low sodium levels, for example, the condition can be treated with dietary salt. In Chapter 9, I will describe a practical method of doing individual specific testing on your pet.

Chapter 3
Conventional and Non-Conventional Cancer Treatments

Your dog has cancer. What are you going to do?

Weighing Options

The first possible choice is to do nothing at all at this point. You could wait until your pet's suffering has reached an intolerable level and then bring his or her life to a close. Another option is to euthanize your dog immediately. I would not recommend either of these courses of action or inaction. No matter how advanced the cancer is, even if there are only weeks left, there are things you can do that can quickly reverse the disease process and greatly extend your dog's life. Simply switching to healthy food, for example, can produce rapid and dramatic results.

As part of making this decision, you may want to consider what the normal life expectancy of your dog is. Life expectancy depends on many things and varies greatly. Just as with humans, no one can accurately predict how long a dog will live. Generally, dogs weighing under twenty pounds live 15-18 years while giant-breed dogs have the shortest life spans – 6-9 years. You can look up the average life expectancy of your dog's breed by performing an internet search, such as "(*your dog's breed)* life expectancy."

If your dog has a tumor and surgery is an option, you should go for that intervention right away, as long as the risks and costs are acceptable to you. Although it won't guarantee a cancer-free future, the advantage of cutting out the present manifestation of disease without delay is obvious. Once the tumor has been removed, you can – and must – follow up with the treatment protocols described in the following chapters to prevent a recurrence. (The same advice applies, of course, to a dog operated on before you discovered this book. Even though he or she may appear healthy, you cannot be certain that s/he has been permanently cured. Further measures, of the kind I describe, must be taken to assure that outcome.)

Whether or not surgery is an option for you, there are some crucial decisions you will need to make without delay.

The first is: are you going to opt for conventional or non-conventional treatment? Conventional treatment includes interventions like chemotherapy, radiation, and pharmaceuticals, all of which are prescribed by a veterinarian. Non-conventional treatment focuses on nutrition, supplements, stress reduction, and other modes of holistic healing. These may be provided by specialist practitioners – or by you, on the basis of personal research.

The factors you would consider in making this choice include cost, effectiveness, quality of life issues, practicality, and assumptions. Let's address these one by one.

Cost

The following chart compares the estimated costs of conventional treatment and those of the non-conventional treatment outlined in this book. Any costs that would be incurred no matter which option you chose (e.g., follow-up veterinary visits) are omitted here. The figures below should be taken as rough guides only; actual costs will depend on many individual and local factors.

Estimated Costs of Treatment (6 months)

Conventional		Non-Conventional	
Radiation		*Food*	
$2,000 - $6,000		$900*	
Chemotherapy		*Supplements*	
$2,000		$300 - $800	
Pain Medication			
$240			
Antibiotics, other meds			
$240			
Total		Total	
$4,480 - $8,480		$1,200 - $1,700	

* Estimated cost of upgrading from standard commercial pet food to high-quality food.

Effectiveness

In assessing effectiveness, one must be alert to the way terminology is used by veterinarians. In vet speak, a dog with lymphoma is considered "cured" by conventional treatment if it survives eight months. That means that even if the cancer returns in nine months, the treatment is considered successful and a cure. Less than 20% of dogs who receive conventional treatment live for two years.

So, when you hear that a certain treatment has an 80% success rate, take it with a grain of skeptical salt. That claim is not a guarantee that your dog will live out its normal life expectancy or even live for more than eight months. Though different cancers vary in their treatment outcomes, conventional treatment rarely produces what you and I would recognize as a definitive, lasting cure.

With the non-conventional treatment I gave Fergie, she lived for an additional two years, four months, and eighteen days. Unfortunately, there are few studies that show survival rates for dogs that receive unconventional treatments. Many vets will tell you, however, that they have seen amazing results from such treatment.

One non-conventional treatment, a fermented wheat germ extract marketed as Avemar, has been shown in scientific studies to eradicate tumors in at least 80% of laboratory animals in a short amount of time. This compound is non-toxic and has no side effects. I will be discussing Avemar in more detail in the following chapters.

Quality of Life
Among the side effects your dog may experience with chemotherapy are:

- Decreased appetite, vomiting, and diarrhea, sometimes requiring hospitalization;
- Drop in white blood cell count, increasing susceptibility to infection;
- Hair loss

Additional medications are usually required to treat the above side effects.

Possible side effects of radiation include:

- Hair loss;
- Radiation burn, which resembles a blistering sunburn;
- Inflammation of mucus membranes when the gums; tongue, cheeks, throat, or similar tissue is a target of the radiation (e.g., with nasal or oral tumors). The mucosa may ulcerate or blister;
- Foul-smelling breath (halitosis);
- Drooling;
- Difficulty eating. A small dog could require a feeding tube if a large portion of the mouth is in the target area;
- Dry eye or irritation of the cornea if the eyes are in the target area. Irreversible cataracts and retinal degeneration may develop later with certain types of radiation treatment;
- Potentially fatal delayed side effects such as softening of the spinal cord, scarring of the kidney or lung, and bone death.

Antibiotics and anti-inflammatory drugs that are used to treat these side effects may have side effects of their own.

A New Wonder Drug?

In June 2009, the Food and Drug Administration (FDA) approved the first drug ever specifically developed to treat cancer in dogs: Palladia, manufactured by Pfizer Animal Health, Inc. News reports touted this as a major step forward in veterinary medicine. The drug is said to work by killing tumor cells and cutting off blood supply to the tumor. Pfizer claims that tumors disappeared, shrank, or stopped growing in about 60% of treated dogs in clinical trials.

Palladia was specifically approved for mast cell tumors in dogs. These tumors are most commonly benign and localized (non-systemic), appearing as lumps on the skin; some are cancerous. There are also malignant, systemic types, found in the liver, spleen, gastrointestinal tract, or bloodstream.

At first sight, the report of the new drug was impressive. But closer examination made it clear that Palladia is far from the Holy Grail. The drug may indeed shrink tumors – but only until they start growing again. Palladia is a treatment, not a cure.

Further, dogs with systemic tumors were excluded from the study; only cancerous skin tumors were treated. But, for such tumors, surgery has an excellent cure rate unless the tumor is well advanced. Why would Palladia be used, with its broad array of toxic side effects? Nearly half (46%) of the dogs in the study suffered diarrhea, while 39.1% developed anorexia, 35.6% lethargy, 32.2% vomiting, 17.2% lameness, and 14.9% weight loss.

The non-conventional treatments I will recommend generally have no side effects if the correct dosage and protocol are followed.

Practicality

How do conventional and non-conventional treatments compare in terms of tasks, time, commitment, etc.?

If you decide to treat your dog with radiation, multiple treatments will be needed, the exact number varying by case. You will probably have to bring your dog to the clinic once a week. The dog will be sedated for the procedure.

If you opt for chemotherapy, either it will be administered intravenously in multiple treatments at the clinic or you will be instructed to give pills to your dog at home.

Should your dog suffer from any of the side effects mentioned above, you will likely be administering more medication to treat them.

Non-conventional treatment will require that you commit yourself to the following.

Study. You will need to spend the time to educate yourself about treatment choices. You have already begun to do this.

Treatment. After deciding on a course of treatment, you will need to buy the necessary food and supplements. Some of the supplements can be found in health food stores, while others will need to be ordered either online or by telephone from their respective distributors. You will find details at BDC.

Preparation. You will be spending perhaps fifteen minutes per day on preparing food and administering supplements. (Most supplements can be mixed in with the food.)

Calculation. At first you will need to calculate the appropriate dosages of supplements, based on the weight of your dog.

Record Keeping. I recommend that you draw up a Supplement Schedule showing the dates on which supplements will be administered and the respective dosages. Each can be checked when done, so that you have a complete record.

Assumptions
Conventional and non-conventional approaches are based on diametrically opposed assumptions.

Conventional treatment is based on the assumption that if a tumor is killed at its site with toxic chemicals and/or radiation, the patient is cured of cancer.

Non-conventional treatments are based on the assumption that cancer cells are present in the whole body and not just at the site of the tumor. A cure is effected by enhancing the body's own immune response and creating an environment in which cancer cells cannot survive.

For a more in-depth discussion of conventional vs. non-conventional treatments, see http://alternativecancer.us/conventional.htm

Obtaining a full understanding of the differences between the two approaches to treatment would require a substantial amount of study. And even more time would be needed to learn how they can be applied to your dog. But if your pet already has cancer, you don't have the time right now to devote to such research. (Over the coming weeks and months, you may have the opportunity to educate yourself more.) The purpose of this book is to get you started on the path of curing your dog with non-conventional treatment in as little time as possible.

I advise you not to try conventional treatments before you have put non-conventional treatments to the test. The former weaken the immune system and poison the body. Does that sound like the result you are seeking? Non-conventional treatment will have a far greater probability of success if your dog's health has not been previously compromised by chemotherapy or radiation.

However, if non-conventional treatment for some reason proves ineffective, you could then resort to the more brutal conventional alternatives, hoping for the best.

There are many non-conventional treatments for cancer. I have sifted those that are, in my opinion, the most effective and practical ones for treating dogs, bearing in mind the important considerations of safety, practicality and cost.

There are cures you may find in your own research that I have intentionally left out of my recommendations because they impose unacceptable inconvenience or expense. For example, a very effective alternative treatment called Cancell or Protocell must be given every four hours for the duration of a dog's life. Few owners could sustain that kind of regimen – and you don't need to be among them. There are many excellent options for healing that are compatible with your regular lifestyle.

Now that you have some essential background, we are ready to get down to our task of restoring your dog to vibrant health.

Let's go!

Chapter 4
Step 1: Remove Poisons

In this and the following chapters, I will outline an array of treatments in order of effectiveness. You are free to implement any or all of them. However, whatever else you choose to do, you need to follow the advice in this chapter. Your dog cannot survive poison. More information and links to the products discussed can be found at BDC.

In Chapter 9, I will give you a method for determining which combination of remedies will work best for your dog. You do not have to use this method, but at least you should know that it's available in the event that the selection process seems too daunting.

Dog and human cancers are similar in many respects. We also share with dogs toxic environments that contribute to the development of cancer. We drink the same water, breathe the same air, and are exposed to the same household chemicals as our dogs.

On the other hand, we eat different food and are not exposed as much to pesticides, fertilizers, and other chemicals on the ground. Fido, sticking his nose in the grass every time he goes outside, exposes himself to harmful pesticides and other toxins. Are signs placed on lawns in your neighborhood after they have been chemically treated? If so, keep your dog away from those lawns!

Commercial Dog Food

The other toxins dogs are exposed to that we are not are found in commercial pet food. That's right, the pet foods purchased and trusted by millions of owners contain ingredients that are banned in human foods because they pose severe hazards to health.

An article entitled "What's Really In Pet Food" at www.bornfreeusa.org/facts.php?more=1&p=359, presents the following facts:

About 50% of an animal is left over after it has been processed for human consumption. These byproducts include the head, feet, bones, blood, intestines, lungs, spleen, liver, ligaments, fat trimmings, even fetuses. They find their way into pet food, animal feed, and fertilizer, as well as many other products.

Some of the toxins that are common in pet food are:

Bacteria. The carcasses of animals whose muscle and humanly edible organs have been removed – as well as animals that have died of disease, injury, or natural causes – are taken to a rendering plant where they are shredded, cooked, and drained of fat and blubber. The dry residue is then ground into meal, which is formed into food pellets for pets.

Because an animal that has died on a farm may not reach a rendering plant for up to a week, the carcass becomes a breeding ground for dangerous bacteria such as Salmonella and E. coli. More than 50% of meat meals are estimated to be contaminated with E. coli.

While cooking may kill bacteria, it does not eliminate certain toxins (endotoxins) that some bacteria produce during their growth. These surviving toxins can, of course, cause disease, yet pet food manufacturers do not screen their products for them.

Drugs. Drugs that are used to treat sick animals or euthanize them may still be present in the pet-food end product. Penicillin and pentobarbital are just two examples of drugs that can pass through the various stages of processing unchanged. Some antibiotics are used in livestock production; these are thought to contribute to antibiotic resistance in humans.

Mycotoxins. Modern farming practices, adverse weather conditions, and improper drying and storage of crops can foster the growth of mold or fungi, which are known as mycotoxins. The pet food ingredients most likely to be contaminated with mycotoxins are wheat, corn, and fish meal.

Chemical Residue. Pesticides and fertilizers may leave residue on plant products. Contaminated grains that are found unacceptable for human consumption by the USDA may legally be used, without limitation, in pet food.

GMOs. Genetically modified plant products are also of concern. By 2006, 89% of the planted area of soybeans, 83% of cotton, and 61% of corn in the U.S. consisted of genetically modified varieties. Cottonseed meal is a common ingredient of cattle feed; soy and corn are used directly in many pet foods.

Acrylamide. This is a carcinogenic compound formed at cooking temperatures around 250°F in foods containing certain sugars and the amino acid asparagine, which is prominent in potatoes and cereal grains. Most dry pet foods contain cereal grains or potatoes, and they are processed at high temperatures (well over 500°F in the case of baked goods). The specific effects of acrylamide formation in pet foods are unknown. Astonishingly, the chemical reaction that produces acrylamide is considered desirable in the manufacture of pet food because it imparts a palatable taste!

Nutria. Have you ever seen this name on a dog food label? Sounds really wholesome, doesn't it? In fact, the nutria is a rat-like rodent found in some U.S. waterways. Nutria are ground whole and put in dog food to increase protein content. The critters may have been dead and rotting for days before they reach the processing plant to be put in the food you buy for your dog.

Did I mention that some commercial pet food manufacturers even put euthanized animals from pounds into dog food? At this point, you are not too surprised?

Melamine. In March 2007, the most lethal pet food in history was the subject of the largest recall on record. Menu Foods called in more than one hundred brands, among them Iams, Eukanuba, Hill's Science Diet, Purina Mighty Dog, and many store brands, including Wal-Mart's. Thousands of pets were sickened (the FDA received more than 17,000 reports), and an estimated 20% died from acute renal failure. Cats were more frequently and more severely affected than dogs.

The primary culprit was found to be melamine, a chemical used in plastics and fertilizers. Melamine had been deliberately added to wheat gluten and rice protein concentrate imported from China, to boost the protein content of these pet food ingredients. Feed for cows, pigs, and chickens had been similarly tainted, and thousands of animals were quarantined and destroyed as a result. The rapid-onset kidney disease that had appeared in dogs and cats was caused by the combination of melamine and cyanuric acid, another unauthorized chemical.

Natural? Organic?

You may think that pet foods labeled "natural" or "organic" are safe. Think again. The definition of "natural" adopted by the Association of American Feed Control Officials allows for artificially processed ingredients that most of us would consider very unnatural indeed. Natural flavors, for example can include chemicals such as disodium guanylate, disodium inositate and monosodium glutamate (MSG). And while the term "organic" has a very strict legal definition under the USDA National Organic Program, companies are often adept at finding ways around it.

The name of a company or product may be used to mislead innocent consumers. Not every brand name containing the word "Natural" or even "Organic" is speaking the truth. You should also be aware that the term "organic" does not imply anything at all about animal welfare. Products from cows and chickens may be organic, in the sense that they are free of chemicals, yet the animals may be raised in enormous factory farms where they are treated as nothing more than production units.

The bottom line is that you need to avoid commercial dog food, period. *Don't ever feed your dog something that you wouldn't eat yourself.* This is especially important if your dog has cancer. He or she needs to be given every possible chance to heal. Commercial dog food works in the opposite direction.

For specific food recommendations, see the following chapters. Sources of safe, pre-prepared dog food can be found at BDC.

Water

The quality of the water you are giving your pet is another important factor to consider, as there are many toxins in tap water. The following information is drawn from the website www.pure-earth.com/chlorine.html

Rain flushes airborne pollution from the skies and then washes over the land before running into the rivers, aquifers, and lakes that supply our drinking water. Any and all chemicals generated by human activity can and will find their way into water supplies.

Liquid chlorine is added to drinking water to destroy bacteria. This method used to be considered both completely safe and highly effective, and indeed it was a major factor in reducing mortality from waterborne pathogens. The formerly prevailing view was reflected in a *New York Times* article that stated, without qualification: "Chlorination destroys all animal and microbial life, leaving no trace of itself afterwards."

This sunny assessment could not be sustained in the face of more recent findings of chlorine-based carcinogens, such as chloroform, in water that had allegedly been purified. Surveys have shown that these compounds are common in water supplies throughout the United States. Epidemiological studies support the hypothesis that chlorine accounts for a substantial portion of the cancer risk associated with drinking water. One 1992 study at the Medical College of Wisconsin estimated that about 18% of all rectal cancer cases were associated with long-term consumption of chlorine by-products. According to Moseby's Medical Dictionary, "Chlorine is the greatest crippler and killer of modern times. It is an insidious poison".

There are other dangers and toxins in tap water. As reported in *New Scientist*, a comprehensive survey of U.S. drinking water revealed that your tap water is likely laced with a wide variety of pharmaceuticals and hormonally active chemicals. The eleven most frequently detected compounds were:

Atenolol, a beta-blocker used to treat cardiovascular disease;

Atrazine, an organic herbicide banned in the European Union that has been implicated in the decline of fish stocks and in changes in animal behavior;

Carbamazepine, a mood-stabilizing drug used to treat bipolar disorder;

Estrone, an estrogen hormone secreted by the ovaries and alleged to cause gender changes in fish;

Gemfibrozil, an anti-cholesterol drug;

Meprobamate, a tranquilizer;

Naproxen, a painkiller and anti-inflammatory linked to increased incidence of asthma;

Phenytoin, an anticonvulsant used to treat epilepsy;

Sulfamethoxazole, an antibiotic;

TCEP, a reducing agent used in molecular biology; *Trimethoprim*, an antibiotic.

Needless to say, if you are giving your dog tap water, you are greatly inhibiting his/her chances of recovery. So what is the best water for you and your pet?

Water in plastic bottles has come under suspicion because polycarbonate plastic leaches a toxic chemical, Bisphenol A (BPA).

Filtered water is the best water you and your pet can drink. There are many types of water filters on the market, ranging in price from $20 to over $1,000. My recommendation is to buy a good filtering system that attaches to your sink. I use one that is installed under the sink, with a dedicated faucet above. It costs about $150 and the filters need to be changed every six months. Such filtering systems are available at any home improvement or hardware store and are can also be found at BDC.

If installing an inline filtering system is not practicable for you, you may want to consider a filter that attaches to your existing faucet. Although these filters are generally not as good as the inline systems, they are still a big improvement over the original tap.

Giving your dog chemical-free water is not an optional step. It's a must if the dog is going to be healed of cancer.

Household Chemicals

Household chemicals are another source of toxins. Because hazardous chemicals such as chlorine are found in almost all standard cleaning products, you will need to become acquainted with the many natural, chemical-free cleaners that are available for floors, furniture, bathrooms, etc. We use one called Simple Green, which does an excellent job. We also use a steam cleaner on our ceramic-tile floor that uses no chemicals. Don't imagine that your ammonia floor cleaner is harmless to your dog. He/she is on the floor way more than you are.

Flea and Tick Products

Commercial flea and tick shampoos, collars, dips, sprays, and "spot on" products all contain cancer-causing agents. Worse yet, the effects are cumulative over time. The more commercial flea products that have been applied to your dog, the higher the probability that he/she will become sick. I cannot emphasize this too much: *you need to eliminate the application of all commercial flea and tick products if you want to keep your dog healthy.*

A 2000 report by the Natural Resources Defense Council (NRDC), Poisons on Pets: Health Hazards from Flea and Tick Products, documented a statistically significant association between exposure to topical flea and tick dips and the occurrence of bladder cancer in dogs.

In 2008, the Environmental Protection Agency (EPA) said it received 44,000 complaints regarding "spot on" pest prevention products. These are liquid pesticides that are usually sold in small tubes and squeezed onto the pet's fur and rubbed into the skin. The reactions ranged from skin irritation to seizures and even death. In April 2009, the EPA announced that it was going to scrutinize such products more vigorously. More information can be found here: http://www.epa.gov/opp00001/health/flea-tick-control.html

If you're still not convinced of the dangers posed by these products, please read *Ticked Off With Dangerous Flea (and Tick) Control Products?* on the blog at www.petside.com

To complicate matters, dogs with weak immune systems and low nutrient levels do not repel insects as well as healthy dogs do. A dog with cancer is more susceptible to getting fleas than a healthy dog.

The severity of flea and tick problems varies greatly by geographic location. We had no problems with fleas and ticks when we lived in Pennsylvania, and did not have to resort to any preventive measures. In Florida, where we live now, fleas and ticks abound. If you develop a flea problem in your home, the cure can be worse than the disease: expensive pesticide treatment for the whole house may expose you and your pet to dangerous toxins. Therefore, prevention is essential.

If you are giving your dog brewer's yeast for fleas, you need to know that long-term use causes liver toxicity. You need to dispense with the yeast.

Garlic can be effective for flea prevention, but you should use only small amounts, as too much can cause a life-threatening anemia (hemolytic anemia). Half a clove per day should be sufficient. You can also consider sprinkling garlic powder in food.

Some claim that a tablespoon of apple cider vinegar added to the water bowl does the trick. This is not a bad thing to do anyway if your dog has cancer, since apple cider vinegar can boost the immune system.

Some other non-toxic products for fleas and ticks can be found at BDC. For example:

Cedar oil is an insect killer and repellant that can be applied inside and outside your house and dabbed on your dog.

Eucalyptus and lavender oil sprays also repel fleas and can be used directly on the dog.

Nematodes and *diatomaceous earth* are non-toxic products that can be applied to your yard or lawn to control fleas. Inside the house, you can spread *salt* or *boric acid* powder, wait a few hours, and then vacuum.

Neem shampoo is natural, non-toxic, and kills fleas.

Shoo Tag is an appliance worn on your dog's collar that produces electrical frequencies to ward off fleas and ticks.

See also, *Flea Killers Are Cat and Dog Killers,* at http://www.mypetnaturally.com/ebooks/FleaKillers.pdf by Pat McKay, which recommends the supplement MSM for flea control.

Pesticides and Herbicides

Our dogs are further endangered by the pesticides and herbicides used in our homes and on our lawns. A common herbicide used to kill weeds, 2, 4-dichlorophe-noxyacetic acid (2, 4-D), has been found to double the risk of canine lymphoma when applied to lawns four or more times per year. The powerful defoliant and herbicide Agent Orange, used extensively throughout the Vietnam War, contained 2, 4-D. Although this chemical is legal for use in the United States, concerns over its toxicity have led to bans on its use on lawns and gardens in Sweden, Denmark, Norway, Kuwait, and the Canadian provinces of Quebec and Ontario.

Another pesticide, allethrin, a common ingredient in home mosquito products (coils, mats, oils, and sprays) and other bug sprays, has been linked to liver problems in dogs, according to a 1989 study by the World Health Organization.

Whenever our dogs go outside and put their noses to the ground, they may be sniffing up these and other dangerous pesticides. Treating your lawn and bug problems with natural remedies will help mitigate this risk. However, depending on local circumstances, it may not be possible to completely reduce exposure to all of these pesticides. You should do the best you can. More information can be found at BDC.

An important consideration when dogs have cancer is whether they should continue to receive vaccinations. In recent years, veterinarians have begun to link serious short- and long-term health problems to vaccination. They include:

Cancer;
Inflammatory bowel disease;
Arthritis;
Chronic allergies;
Autoimmune diseases;
Aggressive behavior;
Hip dysplasia;
Liver, kidney, and heart problems.

Vaccinations should be avoided entirely, or at least limited to those that are absolutely necessary. Our vet refused to give Fergie any more vaccinations after her cancer diagnosis.

I have described the most common toxins to which dogs are exposed in the average American household. In your own home, there may be others, such as cigarette smoke, mothballs, and asbestos. Try to identify these, and take any measures you can to eliminate or reduce them.

In addition to avoiding toxins from this point on, you will need to expel those that have accumulated over the years. Fortunately, this is easy to do.

Liquid Zeolite

Cellular zeolite comes from soils that contain a volcanic mineral called clinoptilolite. It has been used for hundreds of years in Asian countries as a health aid, and more recently in the U.S., in both animals and humans. It is non-toxic and recognized by the FDA as safe.

The honeycomb structure of the zeolite molecule makes it a natural trap for toxins, which are then eliminated in stool and urine without adverse side effects. Heavy metals, pesticides, herbicides, plastics, and even the mycotoxins found in many commercial dog foods are thereby removed from the body.

The scientific research on zeolite, not only as a detoxification agent but also as a cancer preventive and treatment, is impressive. Studies have shown improvement in dogs' overall health status, prolongation of their life span, and, in some cases, shrinkage of tumors.[1] Zeolite stimulated tumor suppressor proteins, blocked growth in several types of cancer cells,[2] and boosted destruction (aptoptosis) of cancer cells.[3]

This product can be purchased online; however, be wary of exploitive pricing. For my personal nutritional regimen, I buy, at a reasonable price, enhanced liquid Zeolite with DHQ (another anti-cancer agent) from a distributor at http://zeoliteliquid.com.

Give your dog 3 drops of liquid zeolite 3 times a day for the first week, then 10 drops 3 times a day for the next 7 weeks. After that, go back to the original dosage to sustain the anti-cancer benefits. Zeolite is best given on an empty stomach, at least 30 minutes before the next meal. If your dog is resistant to taking the liquid from a dropper, add the drops to a bowl containing a small amount of water, which will be quickly consumed.

Your first two bottles of zeolite should take you through the eighth week of treatment, following which a smaller supply will be needed.

Stress
Finally, we come to the toll taken by stress. Your dog is stressed by the disease process itself. You are stressed by the awareness that his or her life is threatened. And your stress, in turn, is picked up by the dog, adding to the primary load. This *must* be addressed, as stress interferes with the ability to heal.

There are many great resources to tap into, from on-line stress relief games through relaxation exercises to CDs of calming music or guided meditation. You will be surprised at how effective these aids can be. But for sustained improvement, you will have to use them every day, thereby benefiting from their cumulative effects. Don't be discouraged if you notice no change the first or second time you listen to a relaxation CD or perform a stress-relief exercise. After a few days, your brainwaves will be drawn into ("entrained" to) the relaxation response. And once you are calmer, your dog will relax, too.

Google searches on "online stress relief," "relaxation CDs," etc. will yield many good leads. You can also learn more at BDC.

There are a number of reliable homeopathic stress remedies for you and your dog. Unlike pharmaceutical products, such as Valium and Xanax, they are free of side effects and toxicity. For suggestions, Google "homeopathy stress."

Bach flower remedies, though not homeopathic in the strictest sense, share some of the principles and methods of homeopathy, including the reliance on "essences" that cannot be detected by standard scientific observation. I recommend the Bach Rescue Remedy, which is available in most health food stores and also from online distributors. This remedy is even made for dogs. The drops rather than the spray are advisable for animals, since spraying into the mouth can be frightening to them.

Exercise is essential not only for the promotion of optimal health but also for the relief and control of stress and anxiety. Extend the walks you take with your dog, seeking opportunities to run and play when you're out together.

When we are most stressed, we tend to devote less, rather than more, time to taking care of ourselves. That's a costly error. Recognize the need to maintain yourself in optimal health and harmony – and see how your dog mirrors your well-being.

Chapter 5
Step 2: The Dog Cancer Diet

The nutritional needs of dogs with cancer are different from those of healthy dogs. Tumors depend on glucose for their survival, and they get it from carbohydrates, so rule number one is to restrict carbohydrates in the diet.

What is needed is a diet with high-quality protein and the right balance of fats. (The one exception to this would be for a dog with pancreatitis, which demands the avoidance of fats.)

One of the most dependable base diets that meet these criteria is the Budwig Diet, which some have called the most successful anti-cancer diet in the world. It was developed by Dr. Johanna Budwig, a German chemist, pharmacologist, and physicist who was nominated seven times for a Nobel Prize in Physiology or Medicine. The information below is drawn from the following website: www.budwigflax.com/Articles/Dr%20Budwig.htm

Thirty years of painstaking research revealed to Dr. Budwig that people who were seriously ill with can-

Dr. Steven Eisen

cer always had low levels of two specific substances in their blood: phosphatides and lipoproteins. She also found that cancer patients typically had a greenish-yellow substance in the blood in place of normal amounts of hemoglobin. This discovery helped to explain why cancer patients were so often weak and suffering from anemia.

A third finding was that, in general, the blood of a healthy person contains far higher levels of Omega 3 essential fatty acids than the blood of someone who is ill.

Budwig speculated that, if just the right combination of nutrients were introduced to cancer patients, the greenish-yellow gunk might be replaced with healthy red blood cells. She began to test this hypothesis, using a combination of organic flaxseed oil and quark, a dairy product common in Germany that is similar to cottage cheese.

She found that after only three months on the flaxseed oil-quark combination, patients began to improve. Tumors shrank in size, strength returned, and blood analysis showed that the infamous greenish-yellow substance did indeed disappear. Phosphatide and lipoprotein levels returned to normal, and red blood cells were once again present in healthy amounts. Budwig was even able to help patients whose doctors had told them to "go home and die."

I recommend the Budwig protocol as the foundation of your dog's diet, but you should substitute plain yogurt (without sugar or artificial sweeteners) for the cottage cheese. The reason for this is that the lactose in cottage cheese may be indigestible for some older dogs. Also, yogurt contains beneficial bacteria, probiotics, which can help the digestive tract maintain a healthy bacterial balance. Organic yogurt is better than non-organic.

The best and most economical yogurt is the kind you make yourself. The process is not difficult, and you can make half a gallon in about thirty minutes. We have used the Yogourmet yogurt maker for years, and it works very well. You can find it for a reasonable price at BDC.

The yogurt's beneficial bacterial count will be much higher if you use the Yogourmet Casei Bifidus Acidophilus Probiotic Yogurt Starter (CBA). Incubate this in the yogurt maker for 20-25 hours (not the 12-15 hours recommended in the instructions). For half a gallon of yogurt, double the suggested amount of yogurt starter to two packets.

It is also best to use organic milk (2%), as it does not contain any hormones. This milk should be heated in a double boiler. The homemade yogurt will stay fresh for over three weeks in the refrigerator.

If your dog has pancreatitis, you will need to use low-fat milk. The enzymes recommended in Chapter 7 will also aid in breaking down fat. If the dog becomes weak, refuses to move much, resists eating, or shows an increase in liver enzymes while on this diet, you will need to put him/her on a water fast for a day or two to eliminate all fats. Then, gradually increase food intake, but do not continue the diet for the time being.

Use the enzymes as recommended in Chapter 7 for one month and then re-introduce the yogurt and flaxseed oil if your dog shows signs of significant improvement while on the enzymes. Continue the use of the other recommended supplements during the month that your dog is off the Budwig protocol.

One of the advantages of this protocol is that other supplements can be easily mixed in with the yogurt and flaxseed oil.

If your dog has liver cancer or any other liver disorder, you should replace the flaxseed oil with a good Omega 3 oil. This is because a compromised liver will not correctly convert flaxseed oil into Omega 3 fatty acids. The Omega 3 oil I recommend is Carlson's Norwegian Cod Liver Oil, which can be found at BDC.

Prepare and use the yogurt and oil combination in the following way:

Mix half a cup of yogurt with one tablespoon of flaxseed oil (or cod liver oil), using a blender, egg beater, or electric hand blender to ensure a thorough blending.

(The best organic flaxseed oils can be found at BDC.) The mixture should be freshly prepared every time and immediately fed to the dog.

To make the yogurt/oil blend palatable, mix it with other food that your dog can't resist.

If you decide to use the Budwig diet, you must feed it to your dog for the rest of his/her life. If you don't, the chances of the cancer recurring greatly increase.

The Budwig mixture must be prepared fresh for every meal and consumed immediately.

I recommend that you prepare the other food for your dog in big batches that you can store in the refrigerator for four or five days. There are many recipes on the internet for dogs with cancer. Use organic ingredients whenever possible, and avoid flaxseed oil, fish oil, yogurt and cottage cheese, as your dog will be getting sufficient amounts of such foods from the Budwig mixture.

Your dog should be given a vitamin supplement such as those found at BDC to ensure it is receiving proper nutrition. (Note: if you are going to use the Avemar treatment discussed in the next chapter, the supplement should not contain vitamin C.)

Of course, dogs vary in their food tastes. For a wide selection of recipes, go to www.dogcancerpatches.net/ Healthy_Dog_Cancer_Food.html

Fergie loved chicken, so we used to chop up some organic chicken and mush it into the yogurt. Here are some other recipes we used:

Chicken Stew
Ingredients:
1 package chicken thighs with or without skin (family pack). Remove and discard skin.
1/2 cup water
4 cloves garlic
1 bag frozen or 2 cups fresh broccoli

Place chicken, water, and garlic in crock pot.
Cook on LOW for 6 hours or until chicken is completely cooked..
Add broccoli and stir.
Before serving, remove bones.

Refrigerate up to 6 days, then discard.

Beef Melody
Ingredients:
2 lbs. ground meat or cubed steak
1/2 cup water
4 cloves garlic
1 bag frozen or 2 cups fresh carrots

Place beef, water, and garlic in crock pot.

Cook on LOW for 6 hours or until beef is completely cooked.

Turn crock pot off and add carrots. Stir.

Refrigerate up to 6 days, then discard.

You can create your own recipes. Recommended ingredients include organic chicken, sardines, organic carrots, parsley, garlic, and a little brown (whole grain) rice.

For dogs suffering from diarrhea, dehydration, heat stress, or physical exhaustion, the following formula is recommended:

2 cups filtered water
1 tablespoon unrefined sea salt
1/4 teaspoon liquid colloidal trace minerals (available at health food stores)
1/2 cup unpasteurized local honey

Dosage: 1 tablespoon per 5 pounds body weight, every 2-3 hours.

Chapter 6
Step 3: Immune Enhancement

It is well accepted that cancer is a disease caused, in part, by suppression of the immune system. When the immune system loses its ability to fight abnormal cells, cancer cells proliferate, causing tumors. Therefore, one of the fundamentals of non-conventional treatment for cancer is to supercharge the immune system. This chapter will show you how to do that.

Avemar

Numerous clinical studies have shown that a remarkable supplement called Avemar, a form of fermented wheat germ, is devastating to cancer cells. This effect of the fermented germ was first suggested in the 1960s by the Nobel laureate Dr. Albert Szent-Györgyi, a Hungarian co-discoverer of vitamin C, but the idea was not seriously taken up by researchers until the 1990s. Since then, they have demonstrated that Avemar acts against numerous cancers, including colon and rectal cancer, head and neck cancer, lung cancer, and melanoma.

One animal study from a peer-reviewed journal showed that Avemar reduced tumor development by

70%, and none of the subjects receiving Avemar suffered new metastases.[4] No toxicity was found in any study.

Avemar is now understood to induce apoptosis, or programmed death of cancer cells, after the first twenty-four hours of use. It also has significant anti-inflammatory effects and supports detoxification, aiding the body in disposing of the dead cancer cells and any toxins formed in the process of apoptosis. You can find more technical background at www.avemarusa.com.

After making its initial debut in Europe, Avemar became available in the U.S. in 2005 under the brand name Avé. You can find Avé for the lowest prices available at BDC.

The supplement is so powerful that, following the removal of toxins, it may be enough *on its own* to cure your dog's cancer. But let's not take any chances. I strongly recommend that you use Avemar/Avé as only one among several tools in the treatment plan for your dog.

While the instructions for administering Avemar to humans recommend that it be taken on an empty stomach, this is not practical for dogs, nor is it crucial.

Avemar should be mixed with a little water, and then with food. Your dog is likely to find a newer product, AveULTRA, to be more palatable because it has less orange flavoring than the original. The following dosage recommendation is for both the original Avemar 0.6 oz and the newer AveULTRA 0.2 oz packets. The dosage is based on your dog's weight:

Less than 25 lbs. ¼ packet per day
25 – 50 lbs.   ½ packet per day
Over 50 lbs.   1 packet per day

I recommend the following schedule:

Administer for 60 days initially, then for 30 days every three months. It is essential to maintain this protocol for the remainder of your dog's life to prevent a recurrence or metastasis of the cancer.

Important Notes: Vitamin C has been shown to negate the effects of Avemar. You must therefore make sure that none of the other supplements you are giving your dog contain Vitamin C. Also, keep the Avemar in your refrigerator to maintain its freshness.

AHCC

I recommend that, along with Avemar, you use another powerful immune-system booster: Active Hexose Correlated Compound (AHCC). The two supplements will act synergistically.

AHCC is produced by combining a number of mushrooms used in traditional Japanese healing which, when combined, creates a very powerful hybrid mushroom.

One of the ways AHCC works is by boosting the activity of natural killer (NK) cells by up to 300%. The NK cells destroy cancer cells. The supplement also increases interferon levels and promotes the activity of T cells and macrophages, all aspects of the immune system. You can find a number of studies on AHCC at http://www.ahccpublishedresearch.com/wwwroot-ahcc/default.htm

There are many AHCC products on the market. The best ones can be found at BDC.

I recommend that you give your dog 1 capsule for every 25 lbs. of body weight in the first 6 weeks. You can break the capsule open and mix the contents with food. After the first 6 weeks, continue with a dose of ¼ capsule per day for dogs 25 lbs. or less, and ½ capsule per day for dogs over 25 lbs. This protocol must be maintained for the rest of your dog's life to prevent recurrence. There are no side effects.

You may want to consider Beta Glucan as a substitute for the AHCC.

Beta Glucan

Beta Glucan is another powerful immune-enhancing supplement, which has been recognized more recently for its effectiveness in treating cancer. Derived from yeast, it binds to cancer cells and kills them. Some have claimed that it is even more effective than AHCC. Following are some quotes from studies of Beta Glucan.

"An immunostimulating agent . . . beta-glucan can inhibit tumor growth . . . reduce tumor proliferation, prevent tumor metastasis."[5]

"In this study, we report that tumor-bearing mice treated with a combination of beta-glucan and an anti-tumor mAb show almost complete cessation of tumor growth."[6]

"The Beta-1,3/1,6 glucans additionally enhance the ability of macrophages, one of the most important cells in the immune system, to kill tumor cells. Laboratory studies have revealed the new MG Glucan is significantly effective at activating Macrophages, and via the Macrophages, the entire immune cascade including T-Cells and B-Cells."[7]

Again, there are many sources from which you can buy Beta Glucan, and the best ones can be found at BDC. You will want 500 mg. capsules. One high-quality product, "Transfer Point Beta," can be purchased for $69.95 for 60 capsules. Go to http://betterwayhealth.com.

The recommended dosage for Beta Glucan is 500 mg. for every 25 lbs. of your dog's weight for the first 6 weeks. If you feed your dog more than once a day, it is best to split the dosage between two feedings. After the first 6 weeks, continue with a dose of ¼ capsule per day for dogs 25 lbs. or less and ½ capsule per day for dogs over 25 lbs. Again, the protocol should be maintained for the rest of your dog's life.

In rare instances, Beta Glucan will cause diarrhea. Reducing the dosage by half will cure this. You can then build up the dosage again gradually, allowing your dog to adapt to it.

Chapter 7
Step 4: Enzyme Therapy

Enzymes act as catalysts for all chemical reactions in the body and are necessary to sustain life. A chronic deficiency of enzymes weakens the immune system. Conversely, enzymes have been effectively used as a natural cure for cancer for over one hundred years.

Twenty-two enzymes are naturally produced in the body, most of them in the pancreas. The capacity to produce enzymes decreases with age.

Cancer cells have a protein coating called "fibrin" that protects them from attack by the immune system. Enzymes can break down this coating, thereby removing the cells' defense and exposing them to the immune system's destructive forces. However, for enzyme supplementation to achieve this feat, an adequate dosage is essential.

Enzymes are also capable of reducing inflammation and pain. They are very effective for many ailments common to older dogs, including joint pain, bruises, heart disease, and arthritis.

A note of caution: enzymes thin the blood and should not be given to any dog with bleeding or clotting disorders, or who is on medication that causes blood thinning.

Enzymes are most effective when taken on an empty stomach, but this need not be a prime concern since any loss of effectiveness when enzymes are taken with food is minor.

Enzymes are a vital component of a cancer treatment program for your dog, provided there are no concerns about bleeding or clotting.

If you would like to study the scientific evidence for enzyme therapy, go to the website of Nicholas Gonzalez, M.D., perhaps the foremost expert on the subject: www.dr-gonzalez.com.

Though there are tasty, chewable enzyme supplements made specifically for dogs, they are, in my opinion, greatly overpriced. The more economical supplements I recommend can be found at BDC.

The decision on which product to buy will depend, first of all, on whether your dog will take solid pills without a problem. You will be giving him or her a lot of these pills – 6-18 a day, based upon your dog's weight. There are many enzyme products available; you can find those I recommend at BDC.

If you cannot give your dog pills, you will need to get enzymes in capsule form so that you can sprinkle the contents into food. You can find these, too, at BDC. The cost is very reasonable.

The daily dosage needs to be split in two. Start with 6 pills or capsules per day (3 in the morning and 3 in the evening), then gradually increase the dosage, as shown in the following chart.

Daily Enzyme Dosage (pills/capsules)

Day	Dog Weight					
	0-19 lbs.	*20-29 lbs.*	*30-39 lbs.*	*40-49 lbs.*	*50-59 lbs.*	*60-69 lbs.*
1	6	6	6	6	6	6
2	6	6	6	6	6	6
3	8	8	8	8	8	8
4	8	8	8	8	8	8
5	"	10	10	10	10	10
6	"	10	10	10	10	10
7	"	"	12	12	12	12
8	"	"	12	12	12	12
9	"	"	"	14	14	14
10	"	"	"	14	14	14
11	"	"	"	"	16	16
12	"	"	"	"	16	16
13	"	"	"	"	"	18
14	"	"	"	"	"	18
15	"	"	"	"	"	"

On the third day, administer 8 tablets or capsules. If your dog weighs less than 20 lbs., continue at this dosage.

If your dog weighs 20-29 lbs., administer 10 pills or capsules on the fifth day and hold at that dosage. For each additional 10 lbs. over 30, you will add 2 pills or capsules to the daily dosage 2 days after the prior maximum was reached. Thus, if your dog weighs 40-49 lbs., an ongoing daily dosage of 14 pills or capsules will be established on the ninth day.

These dosages should be continued through day 30. During this time, look for improved mood, playfulness, and/or increased range of motion or movement. You may notice that the dog develops some flatulence; that is OK.

At the end of the 30 days, reduce the daily dosage by 2 pills or capsules every 2 days until you are down to 4 pills/capsules for dogs under 40 lbs., or 6 pills/capsules for dogs over 40 lbs.

With the diet and supplements recommended in this and the prior two chapters, you will have your dog on the most powerful cancer-fighting program I know. This multi-pronged approach will work synergistically. Many have achieved cures with just one of the strategies I have outlined (diet, immune enhancement, enzyme therapy). But if you have a number of available weapons, why not deploy all of them concurrently to maximize your chance of success?

Now you may be asking, "What about all the other natural treatments I've heard about?" I will be addressing many of those in the next chapter.

Chapter 8
Step 5: Vitamins, Herbs, and Other Considerations

If you decide to implement my recommendations for treatment, you should also give your dog a multivitamin mineral supplement that does not contain vitamin C. (Anything that contains vitamin C, other than vegetables, should be avoided so as not to negate the action of Avemar.) Multivitamins can be found at BDC.

Now, what of the many other supplements that are often said to contribute to the healing of cancer? They are so numerous that I couldn't possibly comment on all of them here, and if you attempted to select the "best" ones on the basis of standard comparison, you would quickly find yourself sinking in a swamp of information.

But you don't have to give up on the project .I'm going to greatly simplify it for you.

In this chapter, I will list, with short explanations, some of the more common herbs and natural supplements that have been used to treat cancer. And in the next chapter, I will give you an easy and innovative method for determining whether a supplement will be helpful for your dog's condition. (The method can also be used to learn the appropriateness of my basic treatment protocols for your individual case.)

Other Supplements

Some of the more common additional supplements that might attract your interest, listed in order of estimated efficacy (i.e., those at the top have, in my opinion, the greatest healing potential for a dog afflicted with cancer), are:

Reishi, shiitake, maitake, and cordyceps mushrooms, These will not be necessary if your dog is on the AHCC supplement described in Chapter 6. AHCC combines the immune-enhancing properties of all these mushrooms, making for a much more powerful therapeutic effect than could be obtained from any of them individually.

Probiotics. Beneficial bacteria that restore normal digestion and absorption of nutrients. Yogurt contains probiotic bacteria, but you may want to consider additional supplementation.

IP-6. Cancer cells have abnormally high amounts of iron; this supplement removes excess iron specifically from tumor cells.

Turmeric. An Indian spice used in curry; contains curcumin, which has been shown to destroy cancer cells.

Astragalus. An herb known for its immune-enhancing properties.

Essiac tea (aka *Flor-escence*). An herbal blend. Sheep sorrel is the primary cancer-killing ingredient.

Melatonin. A natural hormone produced by the body; production decreases with age. Often used as a sleep aid. Because it crosses the blood-brain barrier, has been especially effective in treating brain tumors.

Fish oil (Omega 3 fatty acids). If you are giving your dog the yogurt and flaxseed oil mixture recommended in Chapter 5, that will be providing all the Omega 3's needed. If not, consider adding fish oil to your dog's diet.

Echinacea. An herb often relied on as an immune system booster.

Cat's claw (uña de gato). Another immune-enhancing herb, with antioxidant properties.

Milk thistle. An herb known to protect the liver from toxic damage.

Shark cartilage. Has been claimed to reduce blood flow to tumors, thereby shrinking them.

Wheat grass extract. Provides oxygen to cells and is also an antioxidant.

Co-Q10. Found in every cell in the body; strengthens immune response to infections and certain types of cancer.

Garlic. A natural antibiotic; stimulates the immune system, increasing the effectiveness of white blood cells and T cells.

Licorice root. A Chinese herb that enhances immune response.

Ligustrum, ginseng, codonopsis, atractylodes, and ganoderma. Chinese herbs that enhance immunity.

Homeopathic Remedies
Phosphorus. For cancer of the forehead with an open sore, blood, and pus.

Arsenic album. For leukemia and stomach cancer with burning heat and dryness of skin; thirst, restlessness, apprehensiveness, shortness of breath, anxiety.

Nitric acid. For stomach cancer with burning pain, thirst, water-induced nausea, inability to retain food; vomiting of slime and blood; face yellow, scrawny and emaciated.

Causticum. For pricking pain.

Alumen. For breast cancer.

Alumina. For rectal cancer with constipation and pain after stool.

Ruta. For rectal cancer with pain lasting several hours after stool; also brain tumors.

Apis M.. For stinging pain with itching.

Clematis. For lip cancer. If there is watery growth, alternate with *Dulcamara.*

Sepia. For hardened lip cancer.

Conium. For lip or prostate cancer.

Calendula. For any stage of cancer. Moderates pain and gives comfort.

Hydrastis. For lip or breast cancer with hardening of tumor, wasting; knife-like pain in breast.

Aurum ars. For face or lip cancer.

<u>Note</u>: The selection of supplements is complicated by the fact that, in combination, some may counteract the effects of others. But here again, the evaluation

method described in the next chapter should enable you to make appropriate choices.

There are substances I have intentionally omitted from the above lists for various reasons, e.g., prohibitive cost, need for administration more than twice a day or by injection, excessive side effects. Some I have left out because they are contraindicated if used alongside the treatments recommended in Chapters 5 through 7. Hydrazine sulfate, for instance, should not be taken with cultured dairy products like yogurt.

Dosages

In general, the recommended dose of any supplement for a dog is based on the dose that would be appropriate for a person weighing 150 lbs. Thus, you would divide the weight of your dog by 150, and then multiply the human dosage by the result of that division.

For instance, if your dog weighs 30 lbs. and the recommended dosage for a person weighing 150 lbs. is 100 mg, the calculation would be 30/150 [= 0.2] x 100 = 20 mg.

Energy Treatments

One range of therapies not discussed so far is classified as "vitalistic." These healing methods are based on the principle that the laws of physics and chemistry alone do not explain all the processes of life. There is a vital principle inherent in all living organisms that is distinct from the forces recognized and measured by materialist science. This principle is variously referred to as chi, spirit, soul, life force, and more.

Healing methods based on vitalistic principles include acupuncture, chi gung, chiropractic, homeopathy, applied kinesiology, meditation, yoga, and ayurvedic medicine.

Vitalistic treatments are offered by many veterinarians, but you must make sure that these individuals are properly qualified to perform them. Have they put in years of formal study and obtained certification from a legitimate authority? Too many have not. They prefer to dabble, first in one technique, then another, picking up the basics of each healing art from casual reading and a number of video presentations. Your dog deserves better.

Each holistic specialty within veterinary medicine has an association that certifies practitioners who have met the group's professional requirements. These associations provide listings of qualified practitioners. Among them are:

American Veterinary Chiropractic Association
www.avcadoctors.com

American Academy of Veterinary Acupuncture
www.aava.org

The Academy of Veterinary Homeopathy
www.theavh.org

Chapter 9
Testing

My protocols for dietary change, immune enhancement, and enzyme therapy, as outlined in Chapters 5 through 7, call for only a few straightforward choices by you, including the choice to adopt the protocols to begin with. But the selection of additional supplements for your dog from among the hundreds that are available – including those listed in the last chapter – can be daunting if you rely only on written information and the often-contradictory advice of people who claim to have knowledge of the subject.

Fortunately, as I have indicated, there is a simple way to clear a path through all this undergrowth and arrive at choices that you can be confident about – and that make a visible contribution to your dog's recovery.

The technique involved is a classic example of "muscle testing" or applied kinesiology (AK), which is used by a wide variety of health professionals – chiropractors, holistic physicians, dentists, physical therapists, nutritionists – to find out, first, how the body is functioning and malfunctioning and, second, what action should be taken to address any troublesome issues.

The key principle in AK is that our muscles, as aspects of our larger self (body and consciousness), react differently to true and false statements, as well as to sound and unsound suggestions concerning our well-being. In response to a true statement or a sound suggestion, a muscle will maintain its strength. But try presenting it with a falsehood or an imprudent suggestion, and it will weaken. The muscle, in other words, can be approached as the ambassador of an innate wisdom.

While there are many muscle testing techniques, the one I am going to describe here is known as self muscle testing. I have chosen this method because it can be performed on animals by one person and does not require touching the animal.

Needless to say, AK is mocked by those who need to see solid scientific underpinnings to any claims made about how things work in the world, and who are unimpressed by the studies done to date on muscle testing.

I can counter this skepticism only with my own experience. Time and again, I have used AK with outstanding success, by which I mean that therapeutic interventions endorsed by the test proved to be exactly what was needed by a chiropractic patient, a friend, or a sick animal. In Fergie's case, all the actions I recommend in this book – actions that dramatically prolonged her life – were originally subjected to, and validated by, muscle-testing.

Experiences like mine are dismissed as "anecdotes" by the science police. I would merely point out that if all the health practitioners and patients who recount such anecdotes about AK were gathered together, they would fill a large number of sports stadiums!

Nevertheless, your success in restoring your dog to optimal health does *not* depend on the use of this technique. Please use it only if you are comfortable doing so. If you are not, simply be guided by the fact that, in the previous chapter, I listed the supplements in order of estimated efficacy, i.e., those at the top have, in my opinion, the greatest healing potential for a dog afflicted with cancer. Select up to three of them.

If the issue is that you are reluctant to try your hand at an unfamiliar technique, consider taking your dog to one of the many healthcare professionals who are qualified to perform muscle testing.

Practicing the Test

Muscle testing is easy to learn. Though you may have an initial phase of uncertainty about "getting it right,' that can be quickly overcome. First, practice the basic moves:

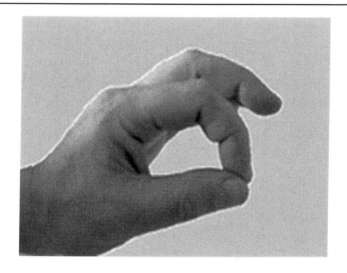

On your *left* hand (if you are right handed; if you are left-handed use your right hand), place the tips of your thumb and index finger together, letting them touch lightly. This will form a space that is roughly the shape of an eye.

Place the index finger of your *right* hand (or left hand if you are left-handed) into the newly formed space.

With a swift motion, swipe the dominant index finger from the base of the thumb toward the meeting point of the thumb and the other index finger, and allow it to break through the connection. Repeat several times.

On the next swipe, sufficiently increase the pressure between the thumb and index finger so that the connection cannot be broken by the dominant index finger. Repeat several times.

Now, "test" the truth of an indisputable statement. Say, "My name is [fill in the blank]," and swipe your dominant index finger. The connection should hold on this true statement. If it doesn't, go back and repeat steps 1-5.

Test the truth of a false statement. Say, "My name is Donuts," and swipe your dominant index finger. The connection should break this time as a result of muscle weakening. If it doesn't, you are holding your fingers together too tightly. Adjust the pressure and try again. (If your name really is Donuts, switch to a different pastry.)

Alternate the true and the false statements until you find that the connection is holding or breaking appropriately *without conscious control of the outcome.* At that point, you will have mastered the technique. Congratulations!

If you are having difficulty with the procedure, the demonstration video at BDC should help you. But if the difficulty persists after you have watched the video and practiced many times, other complicating factors may be at work. For example:

Dehydration. You may be dehydrated and not even know it. The condition interferes with muscle testing.

Physical illness. This would compromise your ability to elicit the response.

Excessive thinking. You need to perform the technique without a lot of mental processing and without letting your ego get in the way.

If none of the above three factors are present, you might have greater success with the following variation of the technique:

Make a fist with your *non-dominant* hand and point your index finger straight out.

Hold the index finger of your *dominant* hand about 2 inches above the other index finger.

Tap the *non-dominant* index finger with the *dominant* index finger, using the same amount of force you used to swipe your finger in the first version of the technique above. If the non-dominant index finger fails to hold its position, the answer is negative.

Using the Test

Now we will use the technique to determine which protocol and supplements are right for your dog. Please follow the instructions to the letter.

Prepare a list of all the substances you want to test.

For each substance, say, "[Name of Substance] will help cure [Name of Dog]'s cancer."

If your swiping finger does not break the connection, indicating approval, write the name of the substance on a second list. Negative responses may be marked on the original list.

To test combinations, say, "[Name of First Substance] and [Name of Second Substance] will together help cure [Name of Dog]'s cancer." Make separate lists of approved and unapproved combinations. Once a combination is approved, you may add a third substance and test again. Larger combinations may also be tested.

Continue this process until you have tested all of the substances singly, and all combinations of those that are approved. You will then have the preliminary list of supplements your dog will need.

You can also test for dosages, length of treatment, and indeed almost any aspect of the treatment plan, as well as for dog foods.

The basic list of substances should be tested every 30 days for the first six months. Supplementation will change as your dog's condition changes. After the first six months, testing can be done every three months.

With these final details of testing, you now have a formidable array of tools to wield against your dog's cancer. Will you succeed in keeping him or her alive? Your chances of doing so have soared as a result of taking seriously the contents of this book, but of course there are no guarantees. No doctor can guarantee a cure for anything, and in fact in most states a health practitioner would be violating the law if she or he did so. There are forces we can control to a degree, and others that we can only respect. One thing is certain: you will do the very best you can for your dear friend, and the bond you share will be strengthened by this odyssey of suffering and healing.

I wish I had known when Fergie was sick all I have since learned about treating canine cancer. I'm convinced that if I could have followed the advanced protocols I have since developed and have presented to you, Fergie would have lived even longer than she did – a heartbreaking thought since every day with her was precious, as I know it is with your dog.

Nevertheless, I am pleased with what I did accomplish. Her life was extended well beyond the expectations of my vet, who sees cancer every day and was astounded by Fergie's exceptional survival. I am deeply grateful for that.

I would have given anything for another day, week, month, or year with Fergie, and I know that you feel the same way about your dog. I have passed on to you whatever I could to make that wish a reality. Now it is only left to you and a higher power.

Chapter 10
A Last Word – to Fergie

Dear Fergie,

It's been well over a year now since I've felt your kisses on my face. I wish you were here to lick off the tears I'm still shedding for you.

Though we now have another sweet dog whom we adore, you are irreplaceable, Fergie. You showed your unconditional love for us through so many years, in ways that felt utterly miraculous.

There was that night when Leslee couldn't sleep because she was in pain, and she tiptoed down to the kitchen to make herself a hot drink. You knew something was wrong, and you came upstairs to wake me so that I could come and help her.

And you would watch over my schedule like the best secretary. You'd wake me up at exactly 8:00 a.m. every Monday, Wednesday, and Friday, the days I had to get up to see morning patients, yet you knew not to wake me on Tuesdays, Thursdays, Saturdays, and Sundays! How did your doggie brain compute that? You were just amazing.

When I looked into your eyes and you looked into mine, it was as if we knew and loved everything about each other. Had you once been a human? Had I once been a dog? Certainly we had some mysterious history that made us intimates.

The night you collapsed was horrendous. Leslee and I rushed you to the hospital, the vets examined you, and they broke the news to us that you had cancer. Then we found out that you had only four weeks to live. We were beside ourselves.

But just as you had taken care of us all of those years, we refused to let disease steal your life away. I barked at the people who told me to "help" you by giving you poisons. Instead, I found good, healthy things that would nourish you back to wholeness. And you thrived and survived. Oh, the joy to witness that!

But can you forgive us for giving you so many terrible things for much of your life? Like the flea and tick chemicals we put on your skin, and that evil dog food that came in a bag? We had no idea back then that they were injuring you. I'm now trying to pull something good from all those mistakes by telling other people about them and spreading the word about how to save dog's lives if they get the illness that struck you.

So many of your brothers and sisters are going to live longer and better lives because of you. And we're so proud of you for that.

Thank you for everything, Fergie.

Till we meet again. . .

Love,

Steve

Endnotes

1   Zarkovic N, Zarkovic K, Kralj M, Borovic S, Sabolovic S, Blazi MP, Cipak A, Pavelic K., Anti-cancer and antioxidative effects of micronized zeolite clinoptilolite., Anticancer Res. 2003 Mar-Apr;23(2B):1589-95.

2   Pavelić K, Hadzija M, Bedrica L, Pavelić J, DikićI, Katić M, Kralj M, Bosnar MH, Kapitanović S, Poljak-Blazi M, Krizanac S, Stojković R, Jurin M, Subotić B, Colić M., Natural zeolite clinoptilolite: new adjuvant in anticancer therapy., J Mol Med. 2001;78(12):708-20.

3   Katic M, Bosnjak B, Gall-Troselj K, Dikic I, Pavelic K., A clinoptilolite effect on cell media and the consequent effects on tumor cells in vitro., Front Biosci. 2006 May 1;11:1722-32.

4   Nichelatti, M. & Hidvégi, M., Experimental and clinical results with Avemar (a dried extract from fermented wheat germ) in animal cancer models and in cancer patients, Nogyógyászati Onkológia, 7:180-185; 2002.

5 Akramiene D, Kondrotas A, Didziapetriene J, Kevelaitis E; "Effects of beta-glucans on the immune system." Medicina (Kaunas). Dept of Physiology, Kaunas U of Medicine, Kaunas, Lithunia. 43(8):597-606; 2007.

6 Li B, Allendorf D, Hansen R, Marroquin J, Ding C, Cramer DE, Yan J; "Yeast beta-Glucan Amplifies Phagocyte Killing of iC3b-Opsonized Tumor Cells via Complement Receptor 3-Syk-Phosphatidylinositol 3-Kinase Pathway." J Immunology: 1:177(3):1661-9. Tumor. Immunobiology Program, James Graham Brown Cancer Center, University of Louisville, Louisville, KY. Aug 2006.

7 Hunter K, Gault R, Jordan F, "Mode of Action of B-Glucan Immunopotentiators-Research Summary Release," Department of Microbiology, University of Nevada School of Medicine, Jan 2001.

<u>NOTES</u>

<u>NOTES</u>

NOTES

<u>NOTES</u>

82936422R00058

Made in the USA
San Bernardino, CA
20 July 2018